Michelle Swyers

Single Parenting

WITH THE FRUIT OF THE SPIRIT

Single Parenting with the Fruit of the Spirit

Trilogy Christian Publishers
A Wholly Owned Subsidary of Trinity Broadcasting Network
2442 Michelle Drive, Tustin, CA 92780

Manufactured in the United States of America

Trilogy Disclaimer: The views and content expressed in this book are those of the author and may not necessarily reflect the views and doctrine of Trilogy Christian Publishing or the Trinity Broadcasting Network.

10 9 8 7 6 5 4 3 2 1
Library of Congress Cataloging-in-Publication Data is available.

ISBN 978-1-64773-748-1
ISBN 978-1-64773-749-8 (ebook)

Dedication

To my ordained parents and grandparents, Major and Mrs. Robert B. Swyers, Brigadier and Mrs. F. M. Gaugh, and Lt. Colonel and Mrs. Walter Swyers, who continually put God first and care for everyone.

To my children, Jack, Kate, and Jess, for filling my life with great joy and meaning.

To my mentor, Martha Tomerlin, for mothering and nurturing me.

To my teacher, Dr. Richard Holz, who believed in me.

To my friend, Wayne Morris, who covered my back with wise counsel.

To Gateway Church in Southlake, TX, thank you for placing value on single parents and helping me to see myself as the Lord sees me.

Table of Contents

Introduction
GOING IT ALONE

You are not a dinosaur! Contrary to what your teen may tell you. You are not prehistoric if you were born before the age of Instagram. The real deal is that you are a single parent who is relevant in the twenty-first century. However, take my advice, and avoid phrases such as *Back in the day*, or *Kids these days*! Just saying!

I know it *feels* like we single parents are not relevant. In fact, the majority of the time, it feels like we are going it alone. That's a lie. If you are a follower of Christ, you are not going it *alone*! You may wish you were alone sometimes. Trust me, I know there are times when all we really want is alone time. However, it is in our moments of solitude that Jesus reminds us that we are influential members of God's kingdom family. We are sons and daughters of the King of kings.

As a member of God's royal family, you are *never* alone! *Never!* In fact, you even have status! You are so significant that you have the authority to transform every environment around you into His kingdom, even in your home! It is important to understand that this is your parental right!

Society often makes us single parents feel like we are less than. More often than not, the church at large politely sets us off to the side in a way that makes us feel like modern-day lepers. It unknowingly sends us the message that yes, we are redeemed, but can no longer do *this*, *that*, or *the other*. For example, singles may not be welcomed to serve as group leaders or church conference speakers.

Thankfully, my church here in Georgia gives single parents positions of leadership. Before moving to Georgia, I attended Gateway Church in Southlake, Texas for many years. They also embrace single parents. Gateway provides special parking places to help single parents with parking needs. Also, at Christmas, Gateway has special shopping sprees for single parents. (God bless 'em!) These churches represent a growing trend among believers that values the contributions of singles parents. Thank goodness!

It is easy to believe lies or have misconceptions about single parenting, so let's get rid of the *big* lies at the beginning. We all want to parent out of fullness and the authority of truth, not from a place of lack and lies. The enemy wants us to embrace a perspective about parenting that is based on deception. So, let's begin by looking at parenting from a kingdom perspective. At the outset, can we just start by debunking a few lies that can distort a Godly parenting perspective?

Maybe you believe that you are a failure because your marriage failed. Perhaps, you believe that you are defined by that and will likely fail at parenting. Not true in the least! Maybe your family or friends rejected you during a divorce. As a result, you believe the lie that no one cares for you. Perhaps, because of this irrational thinking, you feel that you are not worthy of parenting. Not so!

Another lie that so many believe is that you deserve what you get. Perhaps you had a child without being married. You might even worry that you don't deserve to be a legitimate parent or that your parenting can be blessed. Let those worries go. They are lies too. Lies, lies, lies. The truth is, you are defined by Christ's finished work at Calvary. He is victorious, and you are a member of His overcoming family. He has set you up for success. You possess His royal bounty of supplies for your every parenting need.

Because of His mercy and love, the Champion of heaven, Christ Himself, will not fault you. Those family members and friends who *would* accuse you and throw stones at you *can't*. Instead, Jesus, our defender, reminds us all that we are worthy by allowing us to partner with Him to parent our children well.

Thankfully, God doesn't gift us His amazing grace based on our merits or performance. He gives us His grace based on Jesus's merits. Jesus died on the cross for us and for all of our sins and shortcomings in order to bestow an abundantly fruitful life upon us. Jesus took what He didn't deserve in order to give us what we don't deserve. Amen to that!

There are many more lies. Sadly, too many to list. You do not have to go through life believing these lies. You also do not have to parent using a thought process that partners with lies about your lack.

Acknowledging what God does for us and trusting in His plan is the best thing you can do as a parent. By doing so, you can approach your parenting with His numerous provisions from heaven: The Fruit of the Spirit.

Although God's provisions for us are *unlimited*, we will focus on the nine fruits of the Spirit mentioned in Galatians 5:22-23 (NIV): love, joy, peace patience, kindness, goodness, faithfulness, gentleness, and self-control. Trusting in these God-blessed truths will empower us, single parents, by providing us with the energy and much-needed resources to parent and guide our children through life.

> But the fruit of the Spirit is love, joy, peace, patience, kindness, goodness, faithfulness, gentleness, and self-control. Against such things there is no law.
>
> —Galatians 5:22-23 (NIV)

PREPARING THE SOIL OF YOUR SPIRIT
Pulling Weeds & Planting Seeds

You can start your thought process about single parenting by letting God transform your mind right now. First, you need to pull the weeds. On the following pages, list the *lies* that you have believed about what you *don't have*. Then, start planting new seeds as you notate the *truths* that you discovered you *do have*.

LIES THAT I BELIEVE ABOUT BEING A SINGLE PARENT

GOD'S TRUTH ABOUT ME

LIES THAT I BELIEVE ABOUT
FEELING DISQUALIFIED AS A SINGLE PARENT

Michelle Swyers Mitchell, Ed. S.

GOD'S TRUTH THAT QUALIFIES ME
TO BE AN EFFECTIVE SINGLE PARENT

Prologue
LOVE AND SELF-CONTROL

When it comes to the Fruit of the Spirit provisions for our parenting, there are two bookends: love and self-control. Although we will focus on each one of these, it is worth mentioning their special significance and relationship now. It is important to notice that all of the other fruits reside securely in between them. Think of love and self-control like ancient boundary stones positioned first and last. They are in place to give you strength as a single parent. God has established these stones. They are blessed by God.

Curious to know if the decisions you are making as a parent are on track? Check them against these two fixed stones. Take some time to determine if you are leading your family out of love and self-control. If so, you are respecting the boundaries that God established. They are strategically positioned for everyone's blessing and benefit.

"A new commandment I give to you, that you love one another; as I have loved you, that you also love one another. By this all will know that you are My disciples if you have love for one another.

—John 13: 34-35 (NKJV)

Love
ALTOGETHER LOVELY

When we think of the way to lead our children using love, we think of Jesus. He was altogether lovely. In fact, His way of leading His disciples was startlingly simple: "Follow me."

He didn't say, "Follow an impossible set of commands." Rather, He gave a new commandment. A singular imperative. Seriously? Yes. Jesus tells us in John 13:34 (NIV), "Love one another as I have loved you." Or restated for us single parents, *love your children with the love I have given you.*

So how does that work?

Heaven offers us the fruit of love; we just have to be open to receiving it. God provides us with the fruit of love from heaven to share. He does so in a lavish, royal fashion. Parenting begins with God supplying His love *first*. It doesn't start with us "trying" to love others first. This is huge! He is the God of more than enough! So, we have plenty to share with our children.

If your love tank is empty, it doesn't have to stay that way. God created you to continually receive and give love. You function at your maximum as a parent when you deal with this heavenly currency. The best part is that there is an endless supply for your use. Receive it. Give it. Repeat.

You may think the notion of asking God to show you how much He loves you is unrelated to parenting. It is not. Have you ever heard the saying, *hurting people hurt people*? When we feel empty and unloved, we are likely to parent poorly.

Loved people love well! In the kingdom, you have a new name and it's not loveless. God's banner over you is love. God unfurls that mighty truth over you and your family. Stand under it as you parent your children. It's your parental right. This is true because God has positioned you in the love of Christ Jesus and given you the capability to dispense His love to your children.

PARTNERING WITH GOD'S LOVE

Love is a person: Jesus. Love is who He is. Jesus and His powerful love are living on the inside of me. So, parenting out of love is not my own effort. It's Jesus's effort through me. I partner with Him to parent my children well.

Using the tables on the following pages, or another piece of paper, consider how Jesus wants to individually parent your child(ren) with love.

- PERCEIVE: Explain the situation where you perceive that your child needs love.

- RECEIVE: Describe the love that Jesus is freely providing you to meet that need.

- DECISION: Describe how you will partner with His plan to fill that need.

- ACTION: List actions that you are now able to effectively do to share parental love.

Michelle Swyers Mitchell, Ed. S.

	CHILD 1
PERCEIVE[1]	
RECEIVE[2]	
DECISION[3]	
ACTION[4]	

	CHILD 2
PERCEIVE[1]	
RECEIVE[2]	
DECISION[3]	
ACTION[4]	

Michelle Swyers Mitchell, Ed. S.

	CHILD 3
PERCEIVE[1]	
RECEIVE[2]	
DECISION[3]	
ACTION[4]	

	CHILD 4
PERCEIVE[1]	
RECEIVE[2]	
DECISION[3]	
ACTION[4]	

Michelle Swyers Mitchell, Ed. S.

JOY

Joy follows in order after the first fruit of love. Joy is not automatic in our single-parent households. Let's face it, not all aspects of parenting are joyful. Additionally, not all moments in our households are filled with joy.

Anyway, God does have a sense of humor about family life. He doesn't expect us to always have it all together. Let's just say, if people can figure out what your family ate for dinner last night based on the dishes left sitting in the kitchen sink, you may remark, "Joy!" Sometimes, I just say, "Bless this mess," and then go to bed instead. Now going to sleep, *that* is a real joy for single parents.

Trying to get your bundles of joy to clean up the kitchen sink mess? Well, that may also be quite the opposite of a joy-filled moment in the home. At that moment, you might exclaim some word other than, "Joy!"

On that note, let's take some time to appreciate the nourishing value of the fruit of joy. Your kids can only eat from the fruit that is in your house. So, God offers His fruit of joy from heaven for us, single parents, to share with our children. Thank goodness.

This fruit is especially delicious. Seriously! A joy-filled house is like heaven to our children! God provides this fruit to you so that you can have strength! In fact, Nehemiah 8:10 (NKJV) says, "The joy of the Lord is your strength."

> Go your way, eat the fat, drink the sweet, and send portions to those for whom nothing is prepared; for this day is holy to our Lord. Do not sorrow, for the joy of the Lord is your strength.
>
> —Nehemiah 8: 10 (NKJV)

Too many single-parent households are unhappy; this can be due to the circumstances surrounding being a single parent. They are not ideal. But your parenting doesn't have to be marked by sorrow and constantly bemoaning your circumstances. Your children really need to feast on joy and not your sorrow.

You may mourn that you have a broken home. That loss is real. Just understand that our Lord is attracted to those who are mourning, and He offers relief.

Wow, does that mean that if you are mourning that you are an attractive single parent? Yep. That's what God says. See! He really does have a good sense of humor. So, turn over the losses to Him, and He will exchange them for gains. Doesn't that sound like heaven on earth?

After all, He *is* Emmanuel, *Christ with us.* That means our God is with us *always* and in *all ways.* Remember? You're never going it alone. He comforts us with His joy into a place of greater strength so that we become a source of life for our children. That is major! So, you don't have to strive for joy, you just have to receive it from our happy Father in heaven.

COUNT BLESSINGS

Take joy in seeing God's blessings! His comfort increases your strength.

1.

2.

3.

4.

5.

6.

7.

8.

9.

10.

Michelle Swyers Mitchell, Ed. S.

11.

12.

13.

14.

15.

16.

17.

18.

19.

20.

21.

22.

23.

24.

25.

26.

27.

28.

29.

30.

31.

32.

33.

JOY PLAYLIST

Jesus blesses us with the fruit of joy instead of mourning. Think of a few toe-tapping songs that create a joyful mood in your car or house. Here's a few to get started:

- "Oh Sing" — Elevation Worship
- "You Put This Love in My Heart" — Keith Green
- "Be Lifted Higher" — Thomas Miller, Gateway Worship
- "Pennies from Heaven" — Louis Prima
- "Shake Heaven" — Montell Jordan
- "Shackles" — Mary Mary

Add your favorites here:

Michelle Swyers Mitchell, Ed. S.

PEACE

Peace is available to you as you parent your children. The punishing agony of worry and confusion is not for you. If I had to pick only one fruit to receive from heaven as a single parent besides the two main fruits of love and self-control, it would be peace. Peace is a very expensive fruit.

Jesus purchased our peace in order to give it to us. The Bible tells us in Isaiah 53:5 (NIV) that Jesus received the punishment that bought us this fruit of peace. How incredible for Him to bear our punishment for us! How generous of Him to give us peace instead of the burdens of fear and anxiety! What a blessed peace it is!

> ...the punishment that brought us peace was laid on Him,
> and by His stripes we are healed.
>
> —Isaiah 53: 5 (NIV)

This is *the* reason people call it *blessed peace*. It is a terrific blessing to have peace of mind as we parent. It is gifted to us from Jesus. We don't have to receive the burden of a daily beating and punishment from anxiety and worry as we parent. Case in point, you need not lie awake at night distressed with worry because our Lord "... grants sleep to those He loves" (Ps. 127:2, NIV).

Instead, we can seek to receive His limitless supply of peace from heaven. It's a daily choice to eat this fruit. We can choose to receive this miraculous gift. He purchased it to give it to us.

As single parents, His fruit of peace provides us with a sense of security. We can count on this support to face parenting challenges with hope and confidence. As the song goes, "Peace is a promise He keeps." Boy, do I need that assurance daily on a deep level! I am grateful that He continually reminds me of that comfort.

The Lord blesses us with His peace by instilling a deep level of internal assurance and security so that we can be a reservoir of peace to our children. In doing so, we, in turn, provide stability for our kids. Boy, they need daily assurance just as much as we do!

PEACE-BASED OR FEAR-BASED DECISION MAKING

Take a moment to consider God's ultimate plan for your life that demonstrates His fruit of peaceful provision versus your feelings of fearful anxiety. Generally speaking, the parental decisions that I have made out of fear have not gone well. That's because kingdom parenting does not operate out of fearful need. It operates out of peace-centered provision.

Peace-centered provision *feels* like upside-down thinking, and it is. This peaceful mind is from Heaven toward our parental needs. Therefore, be heavenly-minded by embracing the Lord's peace of mind that quells our earthly fears and anxieties. Remember, you don't have to *strive* for it: the peaceful mind is yours!

A mind of fear is from hell. It's hellish. Use this diagram to describe your current thoughts about parenting, both the good and the bad. Describe the fear-based thoughts that trouble you below the line. These are thoughts that cause you confusion and anxiety. Above the line, describe the many heavenly thoughts that the Prince of Peace gifts to us. These thoughts are *not* impressed or intimidated by our parenting fears, worries, and anxieties. For example, *rest* is a heavenly provision, while unrest is a *hellish* thought. Think opposites here!

Fill in the chart on the opposite page with the heavenly and hellish thoughts that are on your mind.

Michelle Swyers Mitchell, Ed. S.

HEAVENLY/PEACEFUL PARENTING PROVISION

HELLISH/FEARFUL PARENTING THOUGHTS

PATIENCE

God never wants single parents to lack patience. This is one area where we need His help the most. Can I get an amen!

The Lord is aware that we need a lot of patience as we parent our children. This is not a surprise to Him. That's why there is an abundance of this fruit for you to enjoy. He's not like us. He's not stingy. He is the God of endless abundance! You honor His son, Jesus, when you graciously receive this fruit from Him in abundance. In an earthly sense, we single parents lack a partner. So, we have losses, gaps, and concerns in the area of parenting. Jesus invites us to exchange them all for gains in the area of parental patience. With kingdom living, we gain all the benefits of patience from a heavenly parent to *overfill* the missing gaps in our story.

> Now, we have received, not the spirit of the world, but the Spirit who is from God, that we might know the things that have been freely given to us by God.
>
> —1 Corinthians 2:12 (NKJV)

You do not need to beg for the gift of patience. You are part of God's family and you are welcome at His banquet table each day. He is not displeased with you for needing to partake of the fruit of patience on a regular basis. In fact, it's quite the opposite! He has prepared the table in advance for you because He knows that you are in need of patience. He is delighted for you to take *freely* from His heavenly patience and to generously give portions to your family as well.

Remember that you are not a servant in heaven's banquet hall. When you receive Jesus, you are no longer a servant but a cherished son or daughter. This intimate relationship is important to understand. You don't have to do things or serve your measly plate of works to the Lord in order for Him to give you a generous portion of the fruit of patience. As if He owes you, based on your effort or works of service.

Literally, God *cannot* give you patience based upon your works and effort! Jesus became a servant and completed His work of redemption at the cross so that God could give you, "richly all things to enjoy" (1 Timothy 6:17, NKJV). Boy, that's generous! That is God. So, feel free to accept His generous gift of the fruit of patience without worrying that it's based upon your merit.

When you lose your patience, you need to understand this truth the most. It's not really lost at all. You can't lose this fruit based upon your performance record! Patience is a God-blessed fruit that has been gifted to us because of Jesus's sacrifice. You can't lose your patience. It is *yours* to keep.

Just because you blow your top as a single parent doesn't mean you're a failure. Why? Because your patience doesn't guarantee that you possess this fruit. Instead, His fruit guarantees that you possess patience. There's a big difference.

Pause and thank Jesus that He provided patience for your every parenting need. Pray that He will help you harness that patience daily, despite the impatient feelings you may have. It is because of Him that you inherited an abundance of patience for your children. In other words, you are rich in this fruit, not poor and starved!

You only starve when you choose to dismiss yourself from the table out of shame because you don't feel like you deserve God's gifts. Don't give Satan a seat at your table. Friend, no one deserves God's fruitful bounty! He offers this gift to us, whether we are deserving of it or not. Jesus paid for it, prepared it, and provided it for each one of us. He delights to share it with you daily to meet your deepest parenting needs. So, bon appétit!

Have you accepted this fruit?

HOLDING THE FRUIT OF PATIENCE
WITH KID GLOVES

Many times, impatience is the result of feeling powerless. Sometimes our irrational feelings get the best of us. This is usually the result of our child disobeying us. We feel indignant and want to exert our authority

Michelle Swyers Mitchell, Ed. S.

to get them to comply. Does that sound like heaven's reality that trains and instructs them on making good choices? Well, it's not.

Heaven's reality gives us the fruit of patient authority over our children in order to help them to be successful in life. When they disobey us, we have divine power from God to lead them towards Him by practicing patience. His version of patient authority is firm in a loving way that protects our children and us. Wow! Now *that* sounds like heaven's reality!

No doubt, impatience may be a short-term solution to get our children to obey. Been there, done that. However, heaven's fruitful way of patient authority allows us to use kid gloves. By kid gloves, I mean the type of patience that your kid needs for certain situations; the kind that promotes a change of heart in your child. Through the Holy Spirit, He empowers us to share an opportunity with our children to receive a change of heart for the long term. That's a blessing! Hey, wait a minute! Does my child get a blessing for misbehavior? Yes. *This* is the gospel! Our wrongs exchanged for His right. This isn't a license to do wrong y'all! Instead, Jesus exchanges all our wrongs for His right. Does that sound like heaven's reality to you? That's because it is.

CHOOSE YOUR FRUIT

You don't have to try to be patient. The Lord Almighty (*El Shaddai, Absolute in Power*) provides this power-packed fruit to us to *be* patient. We parent our children using His gift of patience. The reason why this fruit is important is because God's fruit of patience empowers our children so they can achieve their own unique destiny. Therefore, we no longer need to exert our authority in an unhealthy way or from a point of helplessness. You can stop having a feeding frenzy on this rotten fruit. It just makes you feel awful! Imagine how it makes your child feel!

Look at the two charts on the next page, which represent how the fruit of impatient forcefulness can result in short term compliance, but the fruit of patience can result in a changed heart that is a life-long blessing.

The Rotten Fruit of Impatience

Compliance

Non-Compliance

Powerlessness

Anger/
Impatience

Exert
Powerfulness

Heaven's Fruit of Patience

Change of Heart

Non-Compliance

Exert
Heaven's Way

Powerfulness

Heaven's
Patient
Authority

Michelle Swyers Mitchell, Ed. S.

Take the fruit of patience that the Lord has shared with you and use it. *What is the Lord saying about my child? What are some gifts from heaven that I possess to nurture and empower my child using the fruit of patience?* Fill in the chart below as you think about what heaven's fruit of patience looks like, tastes like, and feels like.

ROTTEN FRUIT	HEAVEN'S FRUIT OF PATIENCE
Shout, huff and puff and blow the house down! *Examples: "You rotten kids!" "I told you all morning to get that room cleaned! Why won't you listen?"*	Using your patience, state reasonable expectations and consequences. *Examples, "You can go out and play after your chore is done." "It's okay with me if you go to the movies with your friends this afternoon, as long as your room is clean."*
Make rash decisions	
Scare your children	
Yell obscenities	
Scream insults or put-downs	
(Fill in your own)	
(Fill in your own)	

Kindness

THE KINDNESS OF JESUS

Jesus lived by kindness. When He demonstrated kindness, He was not too soft. He was assertive, but not overbearing. He was and still is the perfect combination of steel and velvet in flawless proportions. To experience Jesus is to partake in the right *kind* of kindness.

Now, He wants to share this balanced kind of kindness with you as you parent your kids. Jesus wants single parents to have confidence in His perfect kindness. Therefore, His Holy Spirit provides the kind fruit to you to use as you parent.

The fruit of kindness is like Jesus. It is appealing. That makes sense, considering it comes from heaven. This fruit consists of a perfect balance of firmness and give. It feels just right!

When you receive this supernatural, balanced fruit, you know it! Not only does it taste good, but it makes you want to have more. As a single parent, doesn't that sound appealing? After what some of us have been through, couldn't we use a cup of kindness? The Lord knows this, and He never leaves us empty-handed. Never! So, have a cup of His kindness!

THE KINDNESS OF BOAZ

The fruit of kindness looks like *honor*. Ruth 1-4 (NLJV) depicts the story of Boaz and Ruth and illustrates this kind of honor. Look at it this way, the rich older guy, Boaz, is a representation of God. And Ruth? Well, she represents us singles.

Ruth is honored by Boaz even though she is a single widow. He *notices* her while she feels invisible. Doesn't that sound like a description of our Lord? Here's the take-away: you *think* you are invisible as a single parent, but God *sees* you. Honor starts by *seeing*.

Boaz looks after Ruth's safety and protection. Boaz even declares that no harm will come to Ruth! Heavenly kindness does not harm. It simultaneously *protects* your honor and honors by protecting you.

As Ruth follows Boaz and his workers in the fields, Boaz *provides* more than enough grain for Ruth and her mother-in-law, Naomi. Like Boaz, the Lord's kind heart wants you near to Him. His version of kindness honors you by making Himself near and approachable to you. In other words, closeness to Him is where the fruit of kindness is found.

Boaz *welcomes* Ruth to join his company for fellowship and a meal. Doesn't that scream honor? Likewise, our Lord invites us singles who feel neglected and famished to join Him. He will provide His great company and all the fruit you can eat! You are welcomed to sit with Him and partake in His fruit of kindness.

Boaz never sent Ruth away without *blessing* her and supplying her with more than enough to take with her. Imagine Naomi's expression when Ruth arrived home with a bountiful harvest! In the same way, the Lord generously says to us singles, "Open wide your mouth and I will fill it" (Psalm 81:10, NIV).

Even though Ruth was marginalized in the community because she was foreign, widowed, and a woman, Boaz *elevated* her with his kindness. Eventually, he married Ruth. I mean, how *kind* is that?

THE KINDNESS OF SINGLE PARENTS

Single parents who have the fruit of kindness choose honor when it's not required. They live like their kind King, Jesus, *seeing* ways to extend kindness to their children and others. Their kindness guides their family in a *protective* way. They *provide* grace to their children by showing largeness of heart. They are not mean or cruel parents. Instead, they have a kind demeanor that welcomes their children to draw closer.

So, whenever you stay confident in the grace of our King, Jesus, you show kindness as a single parent. Whenever you extend kingdom kindness to your children, who sometimes don't deserve it, you are demonstrating His graceful fruit of kindness. That is, in turn, *blessing* your children. Jesus blesses us with kindness because He can! You can do the same with your children!

For instance, words laced with kindness sound uncommon to your children. Your words of approval are constructive to them. I don't need to tell you that often, our youth, in this text-based culture, speak their minds and blurt out their unkind comments, however destructive they may be. Our children hear enough of this!

In His kingdom, kindness has a place of influence because it does not unleash careless, destructive words. It holds back hurtful and damaging words and instead, like Jesus, blesses because it can. Kindness has standing with the King and uses *elevated* discourse to bring honor to your children. The words you speak as members of His royal family sound distinguished, not coarse. With His help, you can dispense a "velvet and steel" reality of the King's kind resources to your children that build them up and give them hope. That is very appealing!

> Love is patient, love is kind. It does not envy, it does not boast, it is not proud. It does not dishonor others, it is not self-seeking, it is not easily angered, it keeps no record of wrongs. Love does not delight in evil but rejoices with the truth. It always protects, always trusts, always hopes, always perseveres.
>
> —I Corinthians 13: 4-7 (NIV)

GOD'S KIND OF KINDNESS

I honor my children when I

_____

_____

_____

_____

_____

_____

I see my children when I

_____
_____
_____
_____
_____
_____
_____

I protect my children when I

_____
_____
_____
_____
_____
_____

I provide for my children when I

_____
_____
_____
_____
_____
_____

Michelle Swyers Mitchell, Ed. S.

I welcome my children to be close to me when I

I elevate my children when I

I bless my children when I

QUESTIONS FOR YOUR CHILDREN

What are your three favorite ways that I show kindness? (Use this information to honor your children with Kindness.)

Michelle Swyers Mitchell, Ed. S.

GOODNESS

"Safe?... Who said anything about safe? 'Course He isn't safe. But He's good."

—C.S. Lewis, *The Lion, the Witch and the Wardrobe*

While this may seem like a radical precept, if you know in your heart that our sovereign God is good, then there is never a reason for you to be depressed, anxious, fearful, or discouraged as a single parent.

Think about how God's goodness can radically affect your single parenting and your family's future.

✝

THE FRUIT CORE

At the core of every sinful decision that we make is the belief that God is *not* good and that He is trying to keep something from us. Thinking that God is not good can make us depressed, worried, discouraged, and fearful as single parents. That thinking is rotten fruit. It's really, as they say, stinkin' thinkin'. Beware: that rotten fruit wants to be your constant slave driver!

It is possible as a single Christian parent to live with fruitful thinking that is aware of God's goodness. This kingdom perspective does not view parenting the way the world does. At the core of this kingdom perspective, there are two things you must know about God, not just in your head, but at the very core of your whole being! Those two things are that God is sovereign, and God is good.

If we really believe that God is good, it makes sense that we would want to do what He advises as we parent our children. Right? If we really believe that God wants abundant goodness for us, wouldn't we let Him constantly lead us, rather than be driven by our fears and anxieties? So, why do we struggle so often in standing firm in the faith that God is good in all things and in all ways?

While this might seem like a radical precept if you know in your heart that our sovereign God is good, then there is never a reason for you to be depressed, anxious, fearful, or discouraged as a single parent. This type of fear-driven parenting is, simply put, *not* good. God would rather bestow upon you the fruit of His goodness as you parent. He is willing to use His power on your behalf for your good.

No matter what difficulties you face as a single parent (and trust me, I *know* we've got them), realize that God hasn't lost control. Daniel 4:17 (ESV) tells us that, "He rules in the realm of mankind." Not only is He sovereign, but He has *good* planned for our lives and for our children. It is these core beliefs that link with an eternal faith perspective that says, He is in control, and He is good. Trust in His heart of goodness.

God's good perspective of your life has *eternity* in mind! In math, any finite number (like the years of your life span) divided by infinity equals infinity! His perspective is bigger than ours. It's infinite!

> The Most High rules in the kingdom of men.
>
> —Daniel 4:17 (ESV)

> Every good gift and every perfect gift is from above, and comes down from the Father of lights, with whom there is no variation or shadow of turning.
>
> —James 1:17 (NKJV)

GOD'S GIFT OF GOODNESS

Here is God's good parenting perspective! It involves getting off the throne of your parenting and putting God on the throne where He belongs. He hasn't lost control. How could He? He created it all. He's good all the time! Isn't that comforting to us as single parents? Knowing these two core beliefs will infuse your single parenting with His stability for the challenging situations we face.

Without God, it is not possible. He is after our hearts to give us His true heart of goodness for His eternal purposes that are fruitful. So, knowing that God is all-powerful and sovereign is good, but you don't want unlimited power resting in the hands of a cruel God, do you? You have to know in your heart that God is *truly* good!

To recap, God provides His stability in the fruit of His goodness. This fruit helps you face life's challenges as a single parent. He has a big eternal plan in mind for our children and us. The fundamental beliefs that will bless you as you parent are that He is sovereign, and He is Good in all ways, always!

ETERNAL PERSPECTIVE OF
GOD'S GOODNESS

God's good perspective of my life has eternity in mind! He has a big, eternal purpose in mind for my children and me.

What do you think God's eternal purpose is for you as a single parent? How does His goodness to you in the past, present, and future connect with His eternal purpose for your life? Think about these questions, then fill in your answers on the next few pages.

GOODNESS OF GOD IN MY PAST PARENTING

List the ways He has been good.

GOODNESS OF GOD IN MY PRESENT PARENTING

List the ways He is good.

GOODNESS OF GOD IN MY FUTURE PARENTING

List the ways He will be good.

Faithfulness

Give thanks to the Lord, for He is good; His love endures forever.

—1 Chronicles 16:34 (NIV)

One of the most beautiful aspects of God is His faithfulness. His faithfulness endures *forever*. Don't you just love that! In our earthly, human realm, we can't really grasp the full meaning of His faithfulness because we experience so much unfaithfulness.

Let's face it, we can't trust people to *always* be there for us. Spouses leave. Cherished family members die. Our trust cannot solely rest on people because they cannot be reliable all of the time.

We can't put our faith in things either; jobs end, money is lost, tires go flat. I'm stating the obvious, but placing your full trust in people and possessions will leave you wanting. It is God's faithfulness that endures forever.

Eternal faithfulness is hard to grasp. However, it makes sense to trust in God's faithfulness as you parent your children because His faithfulness is permanent, not temporary. The only logical place to put wholehearted trust is in Him. When it comes to parenting, putting faith solely in yourself is not a good strategy. So many say, "Just trust your heart," but God's Word tells us, "The heart is deceitful above all things" (Jeremiah 17: 9, NKJV).

Some people say, "Trust your instincts." This is also not a good parenting strategy for singles. Our knowledge is very limited. Trust me, what you think you see is not all that is there. God is all-knowing; His view is not limited; He sees everything. It is wise to put your faith in Him since He is aware of all the details that you don't see. He doesn't miss a thing.

Can you see how it logically does not make sense to put your trust in any of the things mentioned above? To summarize, people, things, our hearts, and our instincts are just not faithful. Still, we put our faith in these things all the time.

So how do we put our trust in our faithful God to parent our children well as single individuals? This is the parenting strategy that is hardest to grasp. His faithfulness flows from heaven to me and from me to my children. Notice, I didn't say *my* faithfulness flows from me. Not hardly. The fruit of faithfulness from heaven is gifted to me to use for my family. Also, notice how I didn't say, I *try* in my own efforts to be faithful either. That thought is amusing. Neither one of those strategies are His ways. Those are *my* ways.

Look at it this way: you are the steward of His Faithfulness. It's like olive oil. You dispense His fruit of faithfulness the same way you pour oil; you pour it out so that it flows out to your family. It's His, and it's reliable; He gives you authority over it. That is mind-blowingly beautiful and infinitely more satisfying than other temporary strategies.

Beholding God's enduring faithfulness and allowing His forever-fruit of faithfulness to flow like oil from us is what makes us faithful as single parents.

There is an amazing story in the Bible that demonstrates how a king was faithful in a particular situation because he didn't place his faith in himself, other people, things, his heart, or even his instincts. Instead, he focused on how God was the faithful one!

In 2 Chronicles 20, King Jehoshaphat faced a frightening circumstance when three armies came to confront him in battle. The king was afraid, so he decided to seek the Lord. Then, he called everyone together to fast and seek the Lord as well. He stood before them all and told them how faithful God was and that they should put their faith in Him to save them. Then a prophet stood before them and told the people that the battle was not theirs, but the Lord's. Therefore, the king sent the singers out first to sing praises to the Lord and declare that His faithful love endures forever. The enemies became confused and ended up fighting among themselves. It took the king and his people three days to cart away all the valuables. On the fourth day, they blessed God for His faithfulness. In fact, they named the place, The

Michelle Swyers Mitchell, Ed. S.

Valley of Blessing, so they would always remember God's faithfulness.

Let's relate this story into our circumstance of being single parents. Remember the parenting strategy that is seriously hard to grasp: His faithfulness flows from me. If you feel frightened, look to the Lord. Charles Stanley says that all our battles are won on our knees when we seek the Lord. Look in the direction of God's faithful flow! If great numbers of problems face you, put your faith in Him to help with your battle strategy. His faithful strategy flows from you, as you testify to everyone about His enduring faithfulness, despite the appearance of intimidating circumstances. Allow His faithfulness to flow out of you. Accept God's faithfulness so you can face each new day. Let His faithfulness flow like oil out of you.

Having the fruit of faithfulness is not as easy as following steps. It is His faithfulness flowing from me into my family life. It is real and acknowledges feelings to our Father. It surely does not deny the existence of any problems. Simply stated, it is being impressed with our Father's faithfulness flowing like fruitful oil out to challenges that we face as single parents. That fruit from heaven is so simple it is hard to grasp. It feels so good. Let His faithfulness flow like warm life-infused oil running down from wide-open heaven.

TASTING GOD'S FAITHFULNESS

Based on David's *Song of Thanksgiving* (1 Chronicles 16:1-36, NIV), the chart on the following page is a way to remind ourselves of God's faithfulness.

T	*God is faithful in what He does.* In all His _____ works! (verse 9) Because of this fruit, I am _____ as a parent.
A	*God is faithful when we seek Him.* Seek Him and His _____ (verse 11). Because of this fruit, I am _____ as a parent.
S	*God is faithful in His track record.* Remember His _____ works (verse 12). Because of this fruit, I am _____ as a parent.
T	*God is faithful in what He says.* The _____ of His mouth (verse 12). Because of this fruit, I am _____ as a parent.
E	*God is faithful to family legacy.* Remember His _____ for a thousand _____ (verse 15). Because of this fruit, I am _____ as a parent.

GENTLENESS

The Holy Spirit's fruit of gentleness is all about handling relationships with just the right touch. This special fruit from heaven feels like an elevated approach to relating to your children that is full of honor and value.

Although the Lord approaches each of us differently, it is always in just the right way and attends to our individual needs. His gentleness disarms our personal fears and infuses us with warm esteem. Jesus, who is the greatest gift, chose to leave heaven and take on human flesh in order to pursue a close relationship with the whole world. That's gentleness.

Because of this gentleness, we can open up to Jesus and be ourselves without the dread of rejection. Our children want the same approach from us. Hence, the Holy Spirit shares the fruit of gentleness with us to help us establish close relationships with our children.

We don't want to be treated in a heavy-handed way; that makes us reject intimacy. Our children are the same. They desire to be treated with gentleness so that they can show up, be themselves, and form intimate relationships with us where they feel secure.

Because Jesus personally builds a gentle relationship with us, we can show up as single parents and be more like who He is and who He designed us to be. 1 John 4:17 (NKJV) states, "As He is, so are we in this world." In the context of single parenting, just as He is gentle, so are we in our family. For instance, most of the time yelling is not very powerful. Instead, you can answer in a gentle and controlled way. As the book of Proverbs tells us, "A soft and gentle tongue breaks the bone" (Proverbs 25:15, AMP).

> Love has been perfected among us in this: that we may have boldness in the day of judgment; because as He is, so are we in this world.
>
> —1 John 4:17 (NKJV)

AS JESUS IS GENTLE, SO AM I

We need to personally experience this fruit more fully in light of our parenting. Reflect on the gentle spirit of Jesus. Then, consider who you are as a parent because of Him.

JESUS IS SO GENTLE WHEN HE	IN MY PARENTING, I AM LIKE HIM WHEN I

Self-Control

Self-control is one of God's greatest gifts and it involves choice. He loves you so much that He gives you freedom to choose. Have you ever heard the phrase, *the choices you make are the choices that make you*? There is amazing self-management power in the choices we make.

It's a simple concept to manage yourself, but it's not easy. Can I just say that if we could manage ourselves easily, or control ourselves, we would all be trim and rich? Simple right? Eat less calories than you expend. Spend less money than you earn. It may be simple, but it's certainly not easy. Because the Lord wants you to *choose well* as a single parent, He gives you the amazing power of self-management through the fruit of self-control.

Self-control, or self-management, consists of three things: perception, decision, and action. My teen and I recently started taking a defensive driver's education class. While learning about safe driving, it occurred to me that what the instructors were teaching reminded me of the parental decision-making process. For example, there is a lag time when you notice a condition that requires action. That is perception. It takes a moment to notice. For others, it takes longer than a moment. Next, you have to decide what to do. That's when you choose what decision you are going to make. Make a decision. Finally, your body actually carries out the action. You act! Thankfully, these three things do not happen all at the same time or we'd be in trouble.

Through the gift of free will, God allows us to choose how to self-manage as we parent. That's huge! Furthermore, God makes you *well able* to parent by providing self-control to empower you to perceive, decide, and act. If you partner with thoughts of "cannot," you're right. You cannot. Then, just like the 1.5 or so million Israelites in the desert who said, "Cannot," you will not walk into God's promises. This is powerful. God gave His people the power to choose and literally gave them exactly what they chose. Wow! That's almost everybody choosing the "cannot," route! What a scary thought!

However, if you are like the three who chose to align with God's *perception* of "well able," you're right! He makes you fully capable to *decide* and take *action* by stepping into parental territory, inheritance, and legacy that are reserved for the possessors of His promises. Again, the concept is simple, but not easy.

Why did the Israelites choose the "cannot" route? Because, like us single parents, they felt like they were not enough. Their numbers were an enormous 1.5 million, and they still felt that way because they chose to align with the feeling of inadequacy! Not to be redundant, but we are just one single parent. So, you can imagine why it is easy for us to choose "cannot." It's very easy. However, God designed the fruit of self-control to allow you to choose *well able* instead of *cannot*. Therefore, with every step you take, He will secure it as yours. He lovingly sets you up for success to benefit you, your children, and all those around you.

God operates with self-control because He is our loving protector. Self-control is about the choices that align with loving protection that seek to benefit our children. God doesn't lose His self-control because it would harm us in the process. Sadly, when we lose self-control with our children, we harm them in the process. Some parents actually feel justified doing this. Understand *that* it is just not necessary!

There is a big difference between choosing to act and reacting by losing control and behaving badly. The latter may get the job done in the short term, but because it lacks the fruit of self-control, it is not fruitful or beneficial for you or your child. More often than not, it is harmful and frightening. None of us want that for our children.

However, it is important to remember that Jesus was not afraid to act when people crossed the line. You shouldn't be afraid to take action either (when your teen breaks curfew, for example). Jesus's kind of self-control took action in a firm way that was designed with relational benefits in mind. The opposite is true when I lose my self-control and unleash on my child. I may get my way, but it doesn't benefit my child or our relationship.

The culture around you does not often partake in the fruit of self-control. If you take a look around, you will notice that self-control is rare! I mean *really* rare! Some choose to rage. The majority chooses not to do anything. They choose the pitiful "cannot route." This route is like the desert; it's desolate and unfruitful.

In summary, you have two choices: well able or cannot. God gives you the fruit of the Spirit, self-control. He gives you the power to choose. That is, He lets you have the power to self-manage yourself. The choices are given to you! You are well able to align with His will to do well as a single parent. His loving Holy Spirit provides wisdom for perception, decisions, and actions. Our Great Provider provides self-control for everyone's protection and benefit. His way of self-control is simple, but not easy.

WATER OF THE WORD
TO REFRESH YOUR SELF-CONTROL

So here's what I want you to do, God helping you: Take your everyday, ordinary life—your sleeping, eating, going-to-work, and walking-around life—and place it before God as an offering. Embracing what God does for you is the best thing you can do for Him. Don't become so well-adjusted to your culture that you fit into it without even thinking. Instead, fix your attention on God. You'll be changed from the inside out. Readily recognize what He wants from you, and quickly respond to it. Unlike the culture around you, always dragging you down to its level of immaturity, God brings the best out of you, develops well-formed maturity in you.

—Romans 12: 1-2 (MSG)

PRAYER FROM SELF-CONTROL

Below is a New Covenant prayer that prays *from* self-control, not for self-control.

Lord, You are _____
_____
_____.

We praise You for _____
_____
_____.

We thank You for _____
_____
_____.

In unity with your will for our families, we declare _____
_____
_____.

Through your Holy Spirit, we perceive _____
_____
_____.

By Your power, we decide_____
_____
_____.

In faith, we take action by _____
_____
_____.

We decree that because You are with us, we do not go it alone, and we are "well able," to _____
_____
_____.

Michelle Swyers Mitchell, Ed. S.

Biographical Note

Michelle Swyers Mitchell is currently a doctoral candidate at Capella University, specializing in Teacher Leadership. She has been a single parent for ten years. Her background includes a Bachelor of Arts in Religious Studies from Southern Methodist University, a Master's from Indiana University in Education, and an Educational Specialist Degree from Kennesaw State University in Teacher Leadership. Her experience in education is one that includes a wide array of teaching levels and settings. She has taught every grade level from PK-12. Additionally, she has taught in a public school district, a private Christian academy (P-12), and the university setting. Currently, she teaches middle school in Atlanta, Georgia, where she lives with two of her three children. She enjoys leading worship and also public speaking to groups about the goodness of the Lord.

Notes

Image Sources

Grass with Weeds Image (pg 9)

>Flowers vector created by freepik; https://www.freepik.com/free-vector/grass-collection-with-flowers_850100.htm#page=3&query=grass&position=0

Positive and Negative Thoughts Image (pg 29)

>Background vector created by rawpixel.com: https://www.freepik.com/free-vector/mental-health-women-vector_3438035.htm#page=1&query=brain&position=5

CPSIA information can be obtained
at www.ICGtesting.com
Printed in the USA
BVHW091052160921
616889BV00017B/1175